T0132219

AuthorHouse™ UK
1663 Liberty Drive
Bloomington, IN 47403 USA
www.authorhouse.co.uk
Phone: 0800.197.4150

Published by AuthorHouse 09/29/2018

ISBN: 978-1-5462-9882-3 (sc)
ISBN: 978-1-5462-9881-6 (e)

Library of Congress Control Number: 2018911724

Print information available on the last page.

This book is printed on acid-free paper.

authorHOUSE®

Salvage Humanity

Mark John Phillips

SRAKKK...

PLEASE, TAKE ME BACK.

DON'T WORRY. IT WILL BE FUN.

MUAH...

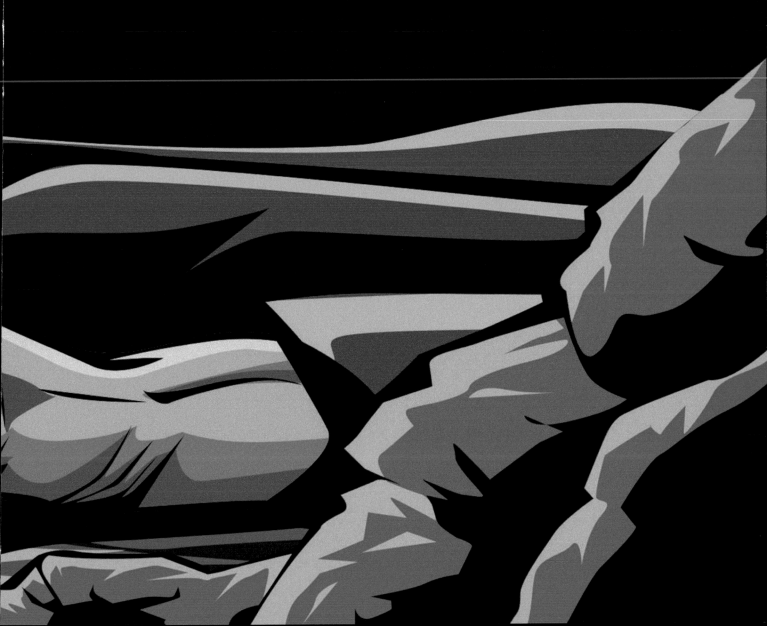

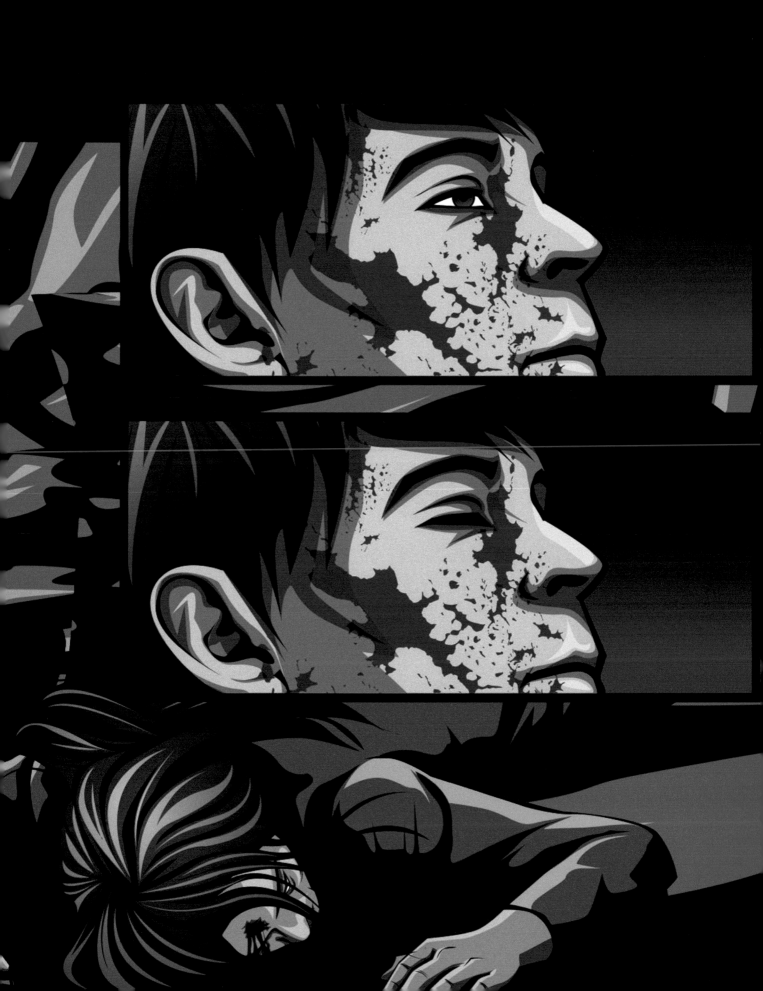

ABOUT THE AUTHOR

My name is Mark John Phillips. I have been a script writer for ten years, writing for myself and for others for their projects. I have also been a filmmaker of my projects for twenty years, behind the camera or in front of it.

I have a good imagination and inspiration. Science fiction is a favourite I like to write about, and *Salvage Humanity* is one of them

So the journey is beginning for me, and so is the story.